A TREASURE OF SMILES COLORING BOOK

BOOK FOUR

By Father Alfred R. Pehrsson, CM

FATHER ALFRED R. PEHRSSON, CM

A TREASURE OF SMILES COLORING BOOK
Book Four

© Copyright 2017 by Father Alfred R. Pehrsson, CM
Registration with the Library of Congress Pending
All rights reserved.

Photographs provided by Father Alfred R. Pehrsson, CM
Editing by Margie Holly Walsh
Paperback ISBN: 978-1981584802

Published by PBJ Enterprises, Inc.
(Precious Blood of Jesus)
Robert T. Walsh, Publisher
162 Liberty Street, Deer Park, NY 11729
United States of America
Email: walsh516@aol.com

This book and others by Father Alfred R. Pehrsson, CM may be ordered in paperback and eBook versions through Amazon.com.

Printed and bound in the United States of America.
First Edition

FATHER ALFRED R. PEHRSSON, CM

A TREASURE OF SMILES COLORING BOOK
Book Four

CONTENTS

FATHER ALFRED R. PEHRSSON, CM

FOREWORD

By Robert T. Walsh
Catholic Publisher
PBJ Enterprises, Inc.
(Precious Blood of Jesus)

This coloring book is part of Father Al's series, "A Treasure of Smiles Coloring Books," for children of all ages to color drawings that provide entertaining reflections of human nature, our relationships with one another and with God. Much of his inspiration comes from a lifetime of dedicated service as a priest in the Vincentian Order.

To better understand what motivates Father Al, we need only turn to the Vincentian Order in terms of its mission, its work and founder, St. Vincent de Paul.

"Our Mission - We follow the call of Jesus Christ to share the good news with the poor, marginalized and abandoned in society.

"Our Work - We serve in multiple missions, parishes and universities in the eastern United States of America.

"Our founder: St. Vincent de Paul, patron saint of charity, founded the Congregation of the Mission 400 years ago in France."

Known as "Vincentians," the Society of St. Vincent de Paul is an international Catholic organization inspired by Gospel values. As such, they provide person-to-person service to those who are needy and suffering. This they do in the tradition of St. Vincent de Paul. United by their spirit of poverty, humility and sharing, they are nourished by prayer and reflection, mutually supportive gatherings and adherence to the basic rules of the Vincentian Order.

Father Al's drawings are yet another way for him to effectively reach out and serve our brothers and sisters in Christ. His books are unique pulpits - the other side of which are congregations around the world who can see his drawings and reflect upon their special messages.

Yes, sometimes a picture is worth a thousand words.

As a Catholic publisher, it gives me great joy to make Father Al's books available through Amazon.com for readers of all ages to enjoy. Praise be the Holy Name of God now and forever.

Bob Walsh
Catholic Publisher
PBJ Enterprises, Inc. (Precious Blood of Jesus)

FATHER ALFRED R. PEHRSSON, CM

ABOUT THE AUTHOR
Father Alfred R. Pehrsson, CM

The war was raging in Europe and in the Pacific. The time was the 1940s. But in our kitchen in Ozone Park, Queens, New York, there was a stillness and peace as we children with our father made imitation drawings of the comic strips of the New York Daily News. As a result, Dick Tracey would often sport a larger hook nose. This was how we Pehrsson family members spent Sunday afternoons. It was togetherness, it was fun and it was creative.

According to my mother, I came into this world on January 17, 1929 during a snow storm. (New York State claims it was on the 18th. I trust my mother's recollection because she was closer to the situation.) With telephone lines down, my father didn't know of my birth for a day and a half!

Old Saint Mary's Hospital in Brooklyn with its ether smell was the place where I first opened my eyes.

My sense-memory of ether has always brought me back to those first moments of someone's greeting, "Well, howdy, stranger. What's your name?"

After the first six years of watching airplanes and the first DC3s fly above us into Floyd Bennett Airfield in Brooklyn, we moved to Ozone Park, Queens. With Aqueduct Racetrack only two blocks away and a race car track beyond Cross Bay Boulevard, it was an exciting place.

P.S. 108 was the place of my first great temptation. To dunk Phyllis Palmer's blonde pig tails into my desk ink well that was conveniently situated immediately behind her ... or not! (You'll never know.)

Mrs. Ryan was my fourth grade teacher. A devout Catholic, and for some mysterious reason, she saw something in her young pupil that which not even my mother saw.

Upon graduating from P.S. 108 in 1943 and having enrolled in John Adam's High School nearby, I received a summons to the rectory of Our Lady of Perpetual Help (OLPH.) Monsignor Flynn informed me that Mrs. Ryan had suggested to him that I receive a parish scholarship to the Vincentian Brooklyn High School of St. John's Prep. Joyfully surprised, that meant I would have the adventure of a daily "El" train ride to the "Bedford Sty" area of the neighboring borough.

Alice Vitelli was the most beautiful 13 year old lass I had ever seen. We met at my graduation party. She was much smarter than I was and therefore went to a special grammar school for brainy kids. In spite of our cultural-educational barriers, Alice made a deal. I could pay 20 cents for us to see a movie Saturday at the Casino Theater if both of us went to the Miraculous Medal Novena at OLPH on Mondays. How could I refuse? It was a good deal.

Mothers are sneaky. They have a way of influencing their sons.

"Alfred, do you like garlic?"

Why no! Anyone in his right mind would say a big negative.

"Well, son, she continued, "if you marry Alice (her family is Italian, you know), you'll be eating garlic for the rest of your life."

If Mom thought this was her best shot, she soon realized she had whetted my appetite for garlic.

Vincentian Father from St. John's University, Father Cyril Meyer, had given the weekly MM Novena at OLPH for 20 years. As I sat next to my love-life each Monday, I became more interested not only in his sermons but also in his ability to reach out to my neighbors. It wasn't the garlic that put a damper on our Saturday afternoon visits to Movie Land but the influence of Father Meyer. He was a Vincentian and I was going to attend a Vincentian High School. No coincidence here.

I am careful with the word "fantastic." However, the 20 or more sons of Saint Vincent de Paul who taught and guided us at the Prep were rather fantastic. As I sat in Latin class, I wanted to be like Father McDonald and his confreres. My fate was sealed between "amo-amas-amat" and "rosa-rosae-rosam." I was to become a priest.

Alice and neighbors attended my "farewell to arms in Ozone Park" party held on John Gotti's mafia turf, Jerome Avenue. There I danced my last "Lindy" with Ginny Otten, my favorite dance partner.

Mom and Dad, teary-eyed, as I was told later, drove me to the Vincentian Minor Seminary of Saint Joseph's in Princeton, New Jersey. The year was 1946 and my dad's 1939 auto with a rope to hold the back door closed, just about made it. Twice a year for the next four years, the old Ford would carry my dear parents over the narrows to Staten Island and beyond.

I enjoyed the camaraderie of 85 young men who had the same desire I did to become a Vincentian priest like Fathers Meyer and McDonald. Friendships forged that September 10th day of 1946 still remain. There are just a handful of us left. A few years ago, we, the remnant, made double eights.

I was very prejudiced with the very name, "Germantown," after experiencing WWII in Ozone Park. But there in G Town was where the Vincentian Mother House (Maison Mere) and Novitiate were located.

In 1950, Saint Vincent's Novitiate offered us, the class of nine, two years of spirituality and Vincentian appreciation. It was the beginning of a pseudo-monastic life that continued for the next eight years. Although tough, I enjoyed it because it was one more step to ordination to the Priesthood of Jesus Christ.

Having taken vows of poverty, chastity, obedience and stability in service to the poor in 1952, approaching by bus, we saw the beautiful Major Seminary of Mary Immaculate, Northampton, Pennsylvania, from a farm hilltop. Six years at MIS deepened our commitment to our mission in life.

"Reverend Mister Pehrsson, as a newly ordained, what would you like to do?"

As a result of my answer, I shipped out of New Yok aboard the Ancon Pan Canal ship three months later. Destination: Panama. Another adventure had begun in 1958 and would last for the next ten years.

On the Atlantic side of the Panama Canal, St. Joseph's parish in Colon was made up of Jamaica-born parishioners with a small number of Chinese. I loved Mrs. Scantelberry's Jamaican accent, "Good night, Fahta! You looka so very pretty tonight." Friendships begun there continue to this day.

In the interior Chiriqui town of David, teaching high school Panamanian boys in the Spanish lingo five subjects a day was the challenge of a lifetime. During this four year period, we "clerical gringos from Brooklyn" brightened up the students' days with our occasional mispronunciations. In 1968, six of us Vincentians closed up shop and upon handing the reins to Spanish Brothers, we all returned to the states.

Adventures in the priestly life continued in Michigan as Retreat Master, Niagara Falls as pastor of Our Lady of Lebanon, Niagara University as Chaplain, Emmitsburg, Maryland, as pastor, Philadelphia on the MM Novena Band and in Alabama as "relief pitcher" for six mission churches. By the way of emails, I maintain contact with many friends I happily met in these missions.

After my legs failed me a few times during the celebration of the Mass in Alabama, it was time to head north to Saint Vincent's Seminary and Saint Catherine's Infirmary in Germantown. I have been here since 2004. It was during this time, that the 1940s Ozone Park kitchen table and the New York News comics prompted me to begin entertaining myself with cartoon drawings. As of this date, August 2017, there are well over 3,000! I do them at night while listening to the TV news. Bringing little boys and girls into existence helps me cope with the crazy world around us.

As an 88 year old and unworthy "alter Christus" (other Christ to the world) I give thanks to God the Father for bringing me into existence during a snow storm in Brooklyn, to God the Son for daily Eucharist, to the Holy Spirit for His mercy poured out with the reminder of … **FORGIVEN, FORGOTTEN, FOREVER**.

All the thanks to my parents, Margie and Al, to the Vincentian Fathers past and present, to Our Blessed Lady who rescued me so very often and to Mrs. Helen Ryan who changed my life forever.

God's blessings on all.
In Jesus and Mary,
Father Alfred R. Pehrsson, CM

FATHER ALFRED R. PEHRSSON, CM

DEDICATION

St. James 1:17, "Every worthwhile gift, every genuine benefit comes from above descending from the Father of luminaries … " even if it is a gift, lowly on the totem pole, that hopefully brings you a smile, namely the gift of drawing a cartoon.

After having preached the Gospel for 50 of my 60 years as a Catholic priest on three continents and while rejoicing in this gift, for my own entertainment and far from thinking of sharing them with others on this scale, I began to bring into existence "little people" with pen and ink. As an 88 year old "retired" Catholic priest I have completed five years of art work often with one eye on the nightly TV news and seasonally, with one eye on the Philadelphia Eagles football team.

The stories with the "little ones" would have died away if it had not been for a wonderful friend of 70 years who saw them in the weekly VINCENTIAN NOTEBOOK, Joe Pritchard of West Islip, New York. Joe encouraged me and spearheaded this project of pen and ink drawings with many of his close friends.

I dedicate this work to the "FATHER OF LUMINARIES," the origin of all gifts.

Furthermore, I thank "Semper Fi" Joe Pritchard and all those whom he enlisted for this endeavor – just as they did for my other books, namely: Joe's niece Patty Sparby, his cousin Jim Coyle, Palma Cortese, Dr. John Egner, Teresa Hansen, Marie Drohan and Father Seth N. Awo Doku. In particular, I extend my heartfelt appreciation to the publishers, Bob and Margie Walsh, who worked tirelessly on this project. Their many talents literally transformed my drawings into the books now available in paperback and eBook formats around the world.

I thank my religious superiors who gave permission for this work. Among my Vincentian confreres there are some who gave adventurous suggestions for the activities of the little people. Heartfelt thanks to them for their wonderful ideas.

Many thanks to the outstanding nursing staff at St. Catherine's Infirmary where I have spent the past four years.

For all those named herein and those unnamed who encouraged this aging son of St. Vincent de Paul, permit me to sing in the name of the "little people," ***THANKS FOR THE MEMORIES!***

God bless you all and everyone.
In Jesus and Mary,
Father Alfred R. Pehrsson, CM

FATHER ALFRED R. PEHRSSON, CM

THE VINCENTIAN ORDER

This is written, September 27, 2017, the Feast of St. Vincent de Paul, on the occasion of celebrating 400 years (1617-2017) of the Vincentian Charism of service to the world's poor as initiated by Saint Vincent, Father of the Poor and Apostle of Charity.

St. Vincent de Paul Biography

If today you were to go to the Pantheon in the Latin Quarter of Paris, France, you would find within its walls statues of French heroes such as Victor Hugo, Voltaire, Alexander Dumas, Madam Curie and Vincent de Paul portrayed in his religious garb. Many in France look upon this humble priest as the "ABRAHAM LINCOLN OF FRANCE," in as much as he freed many poor persons from the enslavement of poverty.

This future Father of the poor was born into a peasant family in a small town of Pouy in southern France in 1581. At the early age of 20, he was ordained a priest. Far from his mind were the suffering poor surrounding him as he strove to acquire a benefice (a permanent Church position with financial benefits) that would provide him with a comfortable life.

Trials and great tribulations molded this self-serving priest such as being enslaved by Barbary pirates who ventured forth from North Africa. During his few years in African captivity, the Lord began to mold him into the apostle who would change the face of France.

Upon returning to his motherland, Vincent gathered a group of ladies in 1617 in order to go out to the poor and infirm of his parish in the village of Châtillon-les-Dombes. (The year 2017 celebrates that event of 400 years ago.) From that moment, his life dramatically changed when he began to realize the close link between evangelization through preaching the Gospel and service to the poor.

The Church in France was being held together only by the working of the Holy Spirit and the promise of Jesus. Humanly speaking, the French clergy was in need of a great reform. Vincent set out to reform diocesan priests with spiritual conferences, spiritual retreats and much needed encouraging support. Banding together, a small community of priests began to preach the Gospel with enthusiasm. It was the beginning of a new blessing on our Church in 1625.

Almighty God showered many talents on His priest. During his lifetime, these talents led St. Vincent to lay the foundation for the Congregation of the Mission in that year of 1625. Presently, there are 4,000 Vincentian priests and brothers serving the poor in 86 countries. We continue this mission of evangelizing the poor by staffing seminaries throughout the world.

With the help of wealthy Parisian women, Vincent established the Ladies of Charity for alleviating the sufferings of the marginalized. With the help of peasant women, he founded the Daughters of Charity that today number 18,000 in 94 countries. Today, the Saint Vincent de Paul Society continues worldwide the work of our founder.

FATHER ALFRED R. PEHRSSON, CM

St. Vincent de Paul, Father of the Poor, went to Our Lord on September 27, 1660 in Paris, France. He was canonized by Pope Clement XII in 1737. Thus the humble peasant of the poor became the saintly Father of the Poor.

In Jesus and Mary,
Father Alfred R. Pehrsson, CM

"SUMMER WITH UNCLE JOE"

MOMENTS IN TIME PHOTOS

Father Al Pehrsson with child lepers in Palo Seco, Panama
Circa 1959

Father Dan Kramer, Father Al Pehrsson, Father Tom Prior and Father
Charles Shanley - Panama City - Circa 1959

Father Al Pehrsson with parishioners in Colon, Panama
Circa 1964

Father Alfred R. Pehrsson, CM
Our Lady of Fatima Shrine
Circa 1985

FATHER ALFRED R. PEHRSSON, CM

Father Alfred C. Pehrsson, CM
Pastor of St. Joseph's Parish
Emmitsburg, MD
Circa 1991

Father Al Pehrsson and other Vincentians meet Pope John Paul II
Circa 2002

FATHER ALFRED R. PEHRSSON, CM

Father Alfred R. Pehrsson, CM

FATHER ALFRED R. PEHRSSON, CM

OTHER SELECT BOOKS
PUBLISHED BY PBJ ENTERPRISES

MIRACLES AT SAINT ANNE'S SHRINE
At St. Jean the Baptiste Church in New York City

By Bob Walsh

The author shares the breath-taking story of miracles occurring at Saint Anne's shrine in St. Jean the Baptiste Church in New York City. The author begins the book with the remarkable story of Saint Anne's life as the mother of the Blessed Virgin Mary, and grandmother of Jesus Christ. What he describes is based upon recorded ancient history, Catholic Church traditions and visions by the saints. Many of the miraculous events described in this book were personally witnessed by the author.

PRECIOUS MEMORIES FOREVER

By John Egner

This wonderful love story was written by John Egner describing the many joys and blessings he and his wife, Patricia Marion Conroy, enjoyed for over 60 years of married life. Here are some of John's own words, "My hope is that readers will appreciate the love, happiness and devotion she gave me and our entire family. This story is about her, our thoughts and feelings. I thank God for her life and the many wonderful moments we shared together. Yes, our many precious memories will live forever."

Books may be ordered in paperback and eBook formats through www.Amazon.com or www.barnesandnoble.com

MY LIFE OF MIRACLES
By Bob Walsh

In this book, the author shares many of the miraculous, exhilarating experiences he has witnessed including countless healings over the course of his lifetime. As he looks back over the years from early childhood to present time, he provides a first-hand account, a "peek behind the scenes," into the reality of God, the angels, the devil and the vast supernatural world that surrounds us all. From his earliest memories in life, he has witnessed God heal people who turned to Him in faith. This includes virtually every type of miracle for the mind, body and spirit in keeping with Christ's words in Matthew 19:26, "With God all things are possible!"

SHE ATE HER SPINACH!
A Love Story

By Joe Pritchard

Those who have had the good fortune to know Joe and Maddy Pritchard can never forget them … and neither will you once you read this wonderful book Joe has written. This love story is about Maddy and the 60 years of married life she and Joe shared together – hand in hand – as they served their family, Catholic parish and local community. This is a touching, heart-warming story built on love, faith and honor.

Books may be ordered in paperback and eBook formats through www.Amazon.com or www.barnesandnoble.com

THE DAY THEY KILLED JESUS CHRIST
A Vision of the Passion
By Bob Walsh

The author writes of the Passion of Jesus Christ as if the reader was personally present to witness the horrific, heart-breaking events as they occurred. The graphic descriptions are strictly based upon information as recorded in the Bible, Catholic Church teachings, studies of the Holy Shroud, visions by the saints and in reported ancient history.

JIMMY'S BOY
Devils, Angels and Miracles
By Bob Walsh

The author shares the true-life story of his childhood experiences when he was regarded as a "blessed child of God" endowed with spiritual gifts. When he prayed for others, God healed people - often in ways that stunned the most skeptical. He was one of 12 children in a poor but devout Catholic family on the east side of New York City during the 1940s and 1950s. Everyone who encountered him - clergy and laity alike - realized he was a special child of God. Unfortunately for him, the devil was also aware.

This first-hand account provides a unique view into the world of devils, angels and miracles that surrounds us all. This book describes in vivid detail the boy's childhood experiences filled with miraculous events and terrifying encounters with evil entities exactly as they occurred. This book is a "must-read" for all believers … and perhaps more so for non-believers.

Books may be ordered in paperback and eBook formats through www.Amazon.com or www.barnesandnoble.com

ENCOUNTERS WITH ANGELS AND SPIRITS

By Bob Walsh

This book presents true stories of encounters people have had with angels and spirits - both good and evil. Some of these stories are ones personally experienced by the author. Hearing these from the perspective of those who lived through them may remind you of similar events in your life. The "good spirits" referred to in this book are angels and glorified souls with God … and those souls who are in Purgatory. The "evil spirits" include Satan, fallen angels and those souls who damned themselves to Hell by living out of God's grace during their physical lives.

GOD'S GUIDE TO LOVE, PEACE AND HAPPINESS

By Bob Walsh

This book presents the very words of God as recorded in the Bible to serve as a guide for us in our search for love, peace and happiness in this life – and in the next! God's words provide a "GPS," a priceless road map, to help us find the best destinations in life. The author addresses the three possible "final stops" at the end of the roads we chose to follow in life. There are roads that lead to the breath-taking beauty of Paradise, or the blessed mercy of Purgatory, or for some, the roads that lead to the never-ending, unspeakable agony of Hell. This is a book everyone should read … before continuing on their journey through life.

Books may be ordered in paperback and eBook formats through www.Amazon.com or www.barnesandnoble.com

CONQUERING THE WILD WEST
EDITH KOHL'S TRILOGY
Three Book Set by Cliff Ammons

LAND OF THE BURNT THIGH
One Woman's Conquest of the Wild, Wild West

THE SODBREAKERS
People Who Lived and Died Settling the West

WOMAN OF THE CAVALCADE
An Epic True Story

Edith Ammons Kohl is one of the talented, brave women who helped to settle America's West. She truly is one of America's unsung heroines. Cliff Ammons, her nephew, now makes available - for the first time ever – all three books written by Edith Kohl, in which she captures the sights, sounds and exciting events actually as they unfolded. She wrote from her personal experiences as she lived it! Her brilliant craft of words describes the grueling, sometimes tragic realities endured by so many in the taming our country's wild, wild West. These historic books are an invaluable treasure that should be required reading for all Americans who value the beginnings of our country.

Books may be ordered in paperback and eBook formats through www.Amazon.com or
www.barnesandnoble.com

FATHER ALFRED R. PEHRSSON, CM

INDEX

FATHER ALFRED R. PEHRSSON, CM

A TREASURE OF SMILES COLORING BOOK
Book Four

YOUR OWN DRAWINGS AND COLORING

FATHER ALFRED R. PEHRSSON, CM

YOUR OWN DRAWINGS AND COLORING

A TREASURE OF SMILES COLORING BOOK
Book Four

YOUR OWN DRAWINGS AND COLORING

FATHER ALFRED R. PEHRSSON, CM

YOUR OWN DRAWINGS AND COLORING

YOUR OWN DRAWINGS AND COLORING

FATHER ALFRED R. PEHRSSON, CM

YOUR OWN DRAWINGS AND COLORING